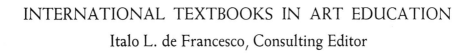

INTERNATIONAL TEXTBOOKS IN ART EDUCATION
Italo L. de Francesco, Consulting Editor

HAND-BUILT POTTERY

Slab pottery — Author.

HAND-BUILT POTTERY

JOSEPHINE R. KRUM

Department of Art
Linden Hall Academy and Junior College

INTERNATIONAL TEXTBOOK COMPANY

Scranton, Pennsylvania

Foreword

This interesting and straightforward account is a record of Miss Krum's experiences and discoveries in the medium of ceramics. It was my pleasure to watch her develop an original and individual style of personal expression as a potter and to see her interest aroused in the use of clay as a potential tool for the teaching of children. I encouraged her to pass on her experiences to other young teachers in the hope that they, too, might share her enthusiasm and insight. I am happy to recommend this little book to those whose task it is to develop plastic expression in young children and who would like to share personally in a fine form of creative expression.

Charles M. Harder*

* Prior to his death in 1959, Professor Emeritus,
  New York State College of Ceramics,
  Alfred University.

Editor's Preface

The making of pottery is among the earliest achievements of man in his struggle to conquer the physical environment. Pottery for the storage of grain, meats, water, juices, perfumes, and other essentials marked a step toward more civilized living. In time, mere "making" became a craft. As the craft developed, it became a means of expression far beyond the original utilitarian purpose.

Our hands are a natural balance wheel. Hands are strong, sensitive, versatile. They are the shaping tools, sensitive to variations in texture and form. For these reasons, pottery making becomes important in sensory and fine arts education.

Most teachers are overawed by the modern equipment needed for pottery; they are also discouraged by the debris and the dust. This book presents a *natural way* of producing pottery and other clay pieces. The basic tools are the hands; other ordinary adjuncts are easily procured. Inventiveness, sensitivity to the material, and a willingness to try are all one needs.

Miss Krum has tried the methods she advocates in her own classroom: with children, with young people, and with adults. She has faith in the methods and in the ultimate success of teachers who are willing to venture.

The work is beautifully illustrated with photographs secured at a great deal of sacrifice. They are a fine complement to an excellent exposition.

Italo L. de Francesco

The Purpose

The purpose of this book is to share an experience and to stimulate a more general use of clay as a creative medium in the classroom. Its plastic nature and the ease with which it can be formed in the hands make clay especially valuable for the development of the tactile and visual senses at the same time.

What the student makes, if he is free to handle clay and find out what it will do for him, will soon begin to reveal his own way of working and take on his individuality quite naturally.

The author hopes that teachers themselves may be persuaded to explore clay, if only to become more familiar with it. There is no better way to understand its potential as a tool for creative education. Further experimentation and actual use of it as an expressive medium will help them to share with their students the intangible but exciting adventure of making something distinctively their own.

What is presented here is not a recipe for working with clay, but a general guide which, to the alert and versatile teacher, will suggest many possibilities and adaptations for particular students and classroom situations. It is understandable that there may not be time and opportunity to explore every idea proposed. However, even the teacher with limited time, space, supplies, and equipment will find how to plan an interesting program of clay experiences for any age group.

Josephine R. Krum

Acknowledgements

The contents of this simple work are largely founded on the personal experiences of the author under the guidance of the late Mr. Charles Harder and members of the faculty of the Design Department of the State University of New York College of Ceramics at Alfred University. Mr. Harder was chairman of the Design Department for many years. His preeminence in the professional field of ceramic design, his experience as the teacher of a generation of fine craftsmen, and above all, his profound and vital interest in the educational potentialities of creative work, encouraged the author, as a teacher of art in the schools, to share this experience with others who work with young people.

To Dr. Italo L. de Francesco, President, State Teachers College, Kutztown, Pennsylvania, the author is indebted, both personally and professionally, for making it possible to make this modest contribution to art education. Dr. Elizabeth Adams Hurwitz, Professor of Art Education, State Teachers College, Kutztown, has constantly encouraged and helped the author with the writing and other details pertaining to the preparation of the manuscript and photographs. Her guidance and understanding will always be deeply appreciated.

The author also wishes to thank her associates at Linden Hall Academy and Junior College, Lititz, Pennsylvania, for their help in preparing the manuscript.

The author is deeply indebted to the many people who in some way have influenced her life. Family, friends, teachers, and students, each in his own way has helped to make this book possible.

Josephine R. Krum

Contents

HAND-BUILT POTTERY

1 CLAY AND MAN

It [the Judeo-Christian view] sees the primary
significance of human life and human civiliza-
tion to be just this: that God, who brought this
mighty creation into existence, has so designed
and ordered it that in the fullness of time the
unfolding drama of its development has pain-
stakingly brought forth within it a creature
with the capacity to understand and enjoy his
creation with Him; a creature by whom and
through whom all creation can at long last
offer praise to, and have communion with,
its Author.

WILLIAM G. POLLARD[1]

Found along creek banks, in swamps,
in lake beds, on river banks, and under
the earth's crust, within the structure of
the sphere, there is a natural material
which we call "clay."

[1] The Cosmic Drama (New York: The National
Council of the Episcopal Church.)

When rain-swollen creeks subside, they leave a residue of clay. Here the clay coats the grasses, leaves, and roots on a creek bank.

Fine particles of clay tend to rise to the surface of the earth after it has rained while heavier particles of rock tend to sink. This soft, pliable clay was once a mud puddle.

Nature is in a continual process of forming clay and providing it in great abundance. Man can find it almost anywhere. Clay, which is taken for granted and used so freely by man, has its birth in the process of making sedimentary rock. It has taken millions of years to make clay, and all the elements of nature have worked together to move and deposit it in the form in which man finds it.

Small particles of rock, almost infinitesimal in size, make up the material. Constant battering by winds and water, as well as other physical and chemical agents, have broken large pieces of rock to the minute size which man finds. Clay contains minerals, silicia and alumina being the two most important. When water is added to these minerals, the tiny particles will cling together and become slippery. When clay is moist, it becomes plastic; that is, it can be made into some shape and it will retain that shape. It has no characteristic shape until man puts it to use in some way, either with his own hands or with a mold. After moist clay has been left to dry, it will keep the same form, and under an intense heat or fire, it will become hard and rocklike.

Sedimentary rock is formed by fine particles of rock that have been broken, moved, and deposited in another place in layers. In time these layers harden into rock. Shales, or "mudstones" are mainly clays, and the layers are visible to the eye. By counting a year for each layer, the age of a deposit can be estimated.

Man's Use of Clay

Man has devised many ways to use clay: as a cup to hold his broth, as a house to shelter him, and as a means to record his history. Its usefulness is still apparent in contemporary society. The first clay objects made by man were baked in the sun, later came the eventful discovery that fire increased their permanence. Knowledge of the possibilities of clay increased with time, but often only through trial and error. Today there are still questions to be answered; for even after centuries a mysterious excitement lies in the interaction of clay and fire.

It is supposed that clay was first used for utilitarian objects. Not only in all the Americas but among all primitive cul-

In the little village of Chinaulti, about a half-hour drive from Guatemala City, women still produce pottery by the ancient method of coil building. The pottery is sold in the markets for daily use in household chores. One woman has just finished the form to the left and is wedging her excess clay. The other woman is still working on her pot and is probably joining the coils together securely.

The pots in Guatemala are carefully stacked on a bed made of pine cones. The cones make an intense heat for firing the ware.

After the cone fire has started, the pots are covered with grasses which will keep the intense heat centered around the pots. These grasses will eventually burn off, making more heat.

The potter adds a handle to her pot. Previously she added the neck and rim to the pot. Her tools are her hands. A small leaf from a bush that has been dipped in water acts as a sponge for cleaning away excess clay. This pot will be used to carry water from the fountain or stream to the home.

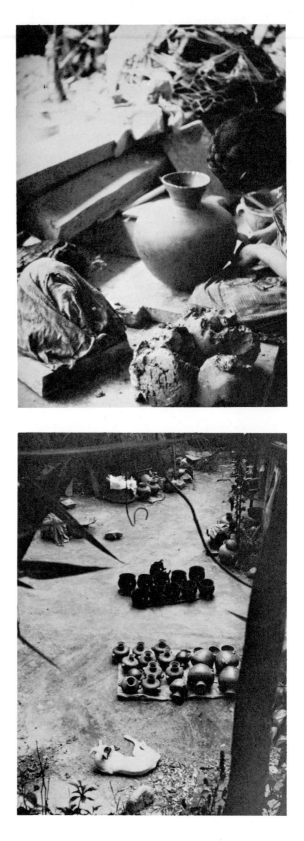

The village in Guatemala is quiet as the work of the week is about finished. The pots have been coiled and are set in the sun to dry. Tomorrow they will be fired and then taken to market to be sold or traded for some other product.

tures, pottery was made by the simple hand-building method of coiling. Women were probably the first pottery makers, because pots were the tools of women, and in simple social groups whoever used a tool had to make it. Women dug the clay, prepared it, coiled the vessels, fired them, and finally put them to use in their daily chores. Pottery, like all other craft products, was made chiefly for family use, although some was made for barter and was traded for other useful articles. Because of this, particularly among the American Pueblo Indians, forms as well as decoration spread from one village to another. They were seldom directly copied; rather, they were adapted and blended with other tribes' traditional forms and motifs. Many were decorated with religious symbols, and certain forms were made especially for tribal ceremonies. Religion was so much a part of daily existence that it becomes in many cases impossible to separate the two purposes. Even in the work of digging the clay there were certain rituals to be observed. "In former days, each woman dug her clay with a stick and carried it home in a basket or hide. While digging she spoke to the earth, asking permission, and perhaps leaving an offering, for pueblo people feel that clay and rocks, like animals and plants, have their own feelings, and that man must live on kindly terms with them."[2]

[2] Ruth Underhill, *Pueblo Crafts* (Phoenix, Ariz.: Phoenix Press, 1945), p. 79.

A Zuni Indian woman from New Mexico prepares clay for making pottery by pounding it into small pieces with a stone. She must remove pebbles and other materials which would hinder her pottery making either in the working or in the firing process.

She uses a bowl as a foundation for building and forming the base of the pot. Here she is adding a coil to the piece.

She must be sure her coils are joined securely, and she does this by smoothly sealing them together. Shaping is not done as each coil is put on, but is done after several have been added. In many cases the shaping is not done until the whole pot has been coiled.

She decorates the pot with kaolin clay which has been mixed with water to form a clip of cream-like thickness. The lower part is decorated with a brown or black slip. Her brushes are parts of the yucca leaf.

The Zuni woman builds a new oven, or kiln, every time she has pottery to fire. Without this firing the pottery would not be durable. She first builds a small fire to warm the pieces. They would crack if they had sudden intense heat applied to them. She then places the pots on old potsherds (broken pieces of pottery which have been fired) raising them from the ground. She makes her oven wall with stones and the roof with potsherds. Cedar bark is pushed under the pots for kindling; sheep or cow dung is used for the main heating fuel. She knows the exact amount of fuel she needs for the length of time the pottery must be fired. The time of firing may vary from one-half hour to two hours. Usually the pots are left to cool slowly and will not be removed from the oven until the next day.

The surface of a Zuni pot is divided into sections for decorating. Each division contains a separate design of a bird or an animal. The neck has a smaller geometric design and the side and neck are divided or separated by one or two strong lines which are broken at one spot; this is said to be for the maker's spirit to escape.

11

Human figures of clay. The large one is 9 inches high — Campeche, Mexico.

Jar — Arkansas.

Burial in a Spiro Indian mound excavated by the University of Oklahoma, Norman, Oklahoma.

Pottery from the Spiro Indian mound excavated by the University of Oklahoma, Norman, Oklahoma.

The history of a people is written clearly in the pottery which they have made. The archaeologist, who looks for information concerning a primitive tribe or a group of ancient people, will find some of his most reliable answers in the potsherds. Specific forms, shapes, or designs can be identified with particular times; for styles had as much meaning for ancient peoples as they do for man today. Decorations on vessels illustrate the life of the people who made them, the clothes they wore, their ways of working, their play, how they made war and peace, what they ate and drank, and how they worshipped their gods.

Clay in History and Literature

As we search the writing of early people, the poets, the historians and the prophets, we discover many who wrote about clay; some wrote of the potter and his work, while others thought of the potter as a symbol of man's purpose in life and a way of living. Of the many Biblical references this is but one:

> Hath not the potter power over
>   the clay;
> Of the same lump to make one
>   vessel
> Unto honour and another unto
>   dishonour?   ROMANS 9:21

This speaks not only of the potter's craft but of life itself: man's privilege to be selective, to make decisions, and to hold to his own beliefs. As the potter considers and determines the growth and final form of each thing he makes from clay, so does man make decisions concerning his own thoughts and actions; these decisions help to make him an individual.

II FEELING AND SEEING

The eye and the hand are the father and mother of artistic activity."

RUDOLF ARNHEIM[1]

One must think of the individual as a whole person and understand the means by which he achieves an identity of his own. The identity means the inborn, essential differences which help us to know one person from another. The individual develops identity through personal experiences and from daily associations with his fellow men. Each person he knows and each experience he undergoes leaves something within him, whether it be eventually accepted or rejected. What is accepted or rejected by the individual becomes a part of him, fitting into the pattern of his identity. What is rejected plays a large part in emphasizing the things which are accepted.

[1] *Art and Visual Perception* (Berkeley: University of California Press, 1954), p. 135.

The Physical Senses

All the experiences which aid in the achievement of identity begin with those which spring from the physical senses: sight, touch, smell, taste, and hearing. The one which is least studied and least developed is the sense of touch. The individual knows the difference between hot and cold, shapes and forms of objects, roughness and smoothness, and other tactile qualities because through experience they have become a part of him; they are either agreeable or disagreeable to him. Consciously or unconsciously everyone has an understanding of what "touching" is. This is not a new theory in education but one which Rousseau expressed a need for over 150 years ago. "Although touch is the sense oftenest used, its discrimination remains, as I have already pointed out, coarser and more imperfect than that of any other sense, because we always use sight along with it, the eye perceives the thing first, and the mind almost always judges without the hand."[2] Henry Moore, the noted sculptor, when describing the creative process of a sculptor, makes this observation: "Many more people are 'form-blind' than colour-blind. The child learning to see first distinguishes only two-dimensional shape; it cannot judge distances, depths. Later for personal safety and practical needs, it has to develop (partly by means of touch) the ability to judge

[2] Jean Jacques Rousseau, *Emile*; translated by Barbara Foxley (Ontario: J. M. Dent & Sons, Ltd., 1911), Book 2, p. 103.

roughly three-dimensional distances. But having satisfied the requirements of practical necessity most people go no further."[3]

It is a difficult thing to prevent a child from seeing or smelling, hearing or tasting, although we can, and often do, prevent him from touching. Obviously, there are traditional reasons for the limitations on how much touching can be done. This is to protect the child, as well as to teach him the value of other people's possessions. But how often do we hand or show an object to a child just for the sake of how it feels? Usually it is: See the pretty stone? Look at the beautiful colors. Smell the pretty flower. Hear the sound of the shell? As adults, probably our own sensitivity to the beauty of tactile qualities has not been fully developed; hence, we may hinder development within the child.

When a child desires to touch something he can't reach, he often finds a tool to aid him and to help extend his world.

[3] Henry Moore, "Notes on Sculpture," in Myfanwy Evans's, *The Painter's Object*, edited by Brewster Ghiselin (Berkeley: University of California Press, 1952), p. 73.

The newborn infant clings strongly to his dual identity with the mother; being held, loved, touched by her is vital to his existence. As growth begins, his separate life and outer objects become more meaningful, and his hands will hold, touch, or rub gently the bottle, the toy, the blanket, or a finger. Eventually, hands, feet, faces, and the whole body start exploring, playing in food, mud puddles, and sand, and with stones, bugs, worms, and frogs, rolling in grass, and burying in leaves, hay and sand. The ways through which a child will search to fill this need of touching are endless; often they are even painful; nevertheless, they are inevitable and necessary to him. Then from the period of the first extensive crawling or the first steps, adults begin to place between the child and reality a protective armor of "don't touch." Sadly, this armor is more limiting than we realize. We deny the child the experiences, but we fail, or make no attempt, to fulfill the desires in other ways.

A teacher who is aware of the necessity for tactile experiences will easily remember children who, in a split second, will take in the feel of an object which is forbidden, the eye roving as quickly as the hand that feels, watching to see if anyone is looking. Finally, if touching is continually forbidden, the period is reached when hands stay primarily in pockets. Seldom does the child's desire become strong enough to allow the sense of touch to take its full course. Possibly,

A tentative exploration of a new toy.

Whole bodies start to explore. Making sand angels is just one way.

17

with older children and adults the desire
is there, but the lesson of "don't touch"
is so well taught that desire lies dormant.

*What age will deny themselves the feel of the
sand and the sea?*

Developing the Sense of Touch

Less prohibitive measures are many. We can question within, when we have the urge to cry "don't touch," whether our motives are justified. Are they safety latches? Is it a nuisance to take the time for that moment of experience? We can talk with children in terms of "how it feels," as well as color, taste, or sound. We can become more aware within ourselves of the necessity of knowing "how it feels." If as adults we lack the vocabulary necessary to describe the sensation, we must learn and willingly accept the child's interpretation. Museums where hands can feel as well as eyes can see have now set up materials primarily for the young, who need the tactile experience to complete their understanding of objects. Museums should also set up areas where older students and their teachers would be allowed to touch as well as see objects beyond those of their own making. People who have taken young people on field trips can readily remember the constant reminders that museum objects are not to be touched. If the need for the tactile experience were not unsatisfied, the reminder would be unnecessary. In schools, materials more interesting to the touch should be available to work with; objects varied in shape, size, texture, weight, structure, and surface in the classroom will aid in the development of the tactile senses.

It is equally important that we not disregard or suppress the other senses. See-

The Toledo Museum of Art school sponsors Saturday classes for children where they are given the opportunity to work in different materials. In a special class in clay work, taught by Norman Schulman, young children begin with hand building methods.

ing, tasting, smelling, and hearing are also vital to the growth of the individual, but they will develop more soundly with the added support of the tactile experiences. As Ralph L. Wickiser says,[4]

"This development of all our physical, mental, emotional, psychological, and spiritual faculties to their greatest potential should be the goal of all education. It should involve complete training that does not emphasize or neglect one faculty for another but recognizes that man is a whole being whose functions depend on each other for full development. Under such training all aspects of personality mature and all sides of man's nature function to live the good life."

Importance of Visual and Tactile Qualities

In the arts, the visual and tactile qualities are of especial importance; one sees through feeling and feels through seeing. While each sense can carry its full importance at separate times, in human beings the visual and tactile experiences are usually concurrent, consciously and subconsciously. It is that interconnection which helps us move from one place to another without bumping into chairs, tables, trees, and buildings, and it is by this same interconnection of sensations that we know how to grasp a cup, a glass,

---

[4] *An Introduction to Art Education* (Yonkers, N. Y.: World Book Co., 1957), pp. 51, 52.

or any living thing and we are able to look at an object and know whether it is round or square, rough or smooth.

One becomes acutely conscious, when teaching people through art, of the necessity for developing a sensitivity to the material used, whether it is paint, paper, crayons, wood, metal, or clay. These materials lend themselves to the development of the touch and visual senses, each material serving a specific purpose and filling a need in its own way.

Clay, the substance which the earth yields in abundance, is one material which uniquely fulfills the needs of the tactile and visual senses; its beauty as a human experience lies both in the simplicity and in the complexity of its use. Here the writer deals with the simplest of its many uses, hand-building methods which can be used in any classroom for a better understanding of clay and of the student.

The act of touching helps one to understand not only the texture of the cat's fur but the form of the animal as well. The cat responds to the human touch, and the feeling of affection is mutual.

FORM AND FORMING

Cultural problems cannot be solved only by intellectual processes. We must strike deeper chords to reawaken in every individual the ability to understand and create form."

Form and Forming

With the tactile and visual, there are two other concepts that must be distinguished in order to understand the creative experience; they are "form" and "forming." Forming is the process of doing, or that which the individual feels or senses while he is doing the work; it is the interplay of man, material, and imagination. Form is that which is sensed as the end product by the maker; it is the object which others see and feel when they behold what someone else has made. For simplicity it is safe to say that "forming" and "creating" convey the same

[1] "The Curse of Conformity," *The Saturday Evening Post*, vol. 231, no. 10, Sept. 6, 1958.

meaning. Creating, which is highly individual and varies in degree among people, can mean something and it can mean nothing. It is based on background, inherent qualities, experiences, intellect, ingenuity, and the ability for personal expression. True creativity can be neither contrived nor forced; it is the spontaneous, emotional, and personal expression of the individual. One begins with an idea; then the material, the way of working, intuition, and sensitivity determine the end product. And only the end product can be understood and evaluated by others. Importance lies not in trying to do something which no one else has done; true value lies in the *forming* and in what is achieved in the end form. The latter is the true identity of the individual revealed through his work. Rudolf Arnheim states:[2] "Imaginative form does not spring from the desire to offer 'something new' but from the need to revive the old. It springs from the original view that an individual or culture will take spontaneously of the inner and outer world. Rather than distorting reality, imaginative form reaffirms the truth. It is the unsought result of the attempt to reproduce an experience as accurately as possible."

Forming is the process of doing, or that which the individual feels or senses while he is doing the work.

Form is that which is sensed as the end product by the maker; it is the object which others see and feel when they behold what someone else has made. Nathan McMahon, Potter.

[2] *Art and Visual Perception* (Berkeley: University of California Press, 1954), p. 114.

Skill and Technique

Students, when given the opportunity to work in clay in a creative-education program, will develop skill in handling the material. They will develop their own styles and ways of working or doing things to the point at which they will become automatic. Skill, then, becomes an important part of the forming process; it is necessary to the individual if he is to reveal his identity with the object he has formed. Technique becomes the way to understand the individual's identity as it appears and becomes more definite as the student increases in skills. Procedures, on the other hand, are those things which the teacher shows a student how to do. Usually they are mechanical factors, such as how to glaze a pot or how to wedge clay. However, rigid ways of doing even these things should not bind the student but should become applicable to his way of working. So, skill and technique cannot be identically termed. Technique cannot be taught or shown, and skill must come purely from experience. Skill will then be an individual's natural way of applying his techniques to clay.

Differences in Processes

Consideration and time should be spent to help the student realize and understand the difference between a hand-built piece (coil, slab, pinch, or other type) and one that is produced by industrial processes. Owing to the industrial products which flood the market, students often assume that the processes which are taught to them are identical with the processes used to make the many clay objects which they have in their homes. This is often the reason that they may try to achieve the "cast" appearance in their own work. Often, too, it is the reason for students being discouraged with their own way of working and their results. Here is the moment when the teacher should take time to explain the differences between the industrial processes and hand building; proper understanding will not only help the students understand their own way of working but make them conscious of the industrial use of clay. This pertains particularly to students on the junior and senior high school level.

It is a valid experience, if time is available, for the student who is interested to model a form, make a mold, and cast ware from his own mold. By contrast, it is deceitful to have a student cast from molds which have been made by other people. This does not help the student understand himself, nor does it help the teacher to understand the individual student. Furthermore, identity of the individual and his personal expression in clay as a creative medium is completely lost.

Contrariwise, there is nothing wrong with using molds. In fact, the use of molds is one of the earliest methods of reproduction invented by man. In the earliest stages of making pottery it is known that clay was pressed into baskets to act either as a lining for the basket or the basket was used as a mold to make a desired form. Molds were also used by the Greeks and the Romans. Josiah Wedgwood used the method; his was the first experiment in mass production known to our times. The use of a mold is the process of reproduction which duplicates many pieces of a kind.

Too, explanation of the way of working when using the mold processes should be given. It is a highly disciplined, rational, calculated, and impersonal way of working. It calls for training and experience as distinguished from the highly personal way and results of a student's handwork or that of an individual art pottery craftsman.

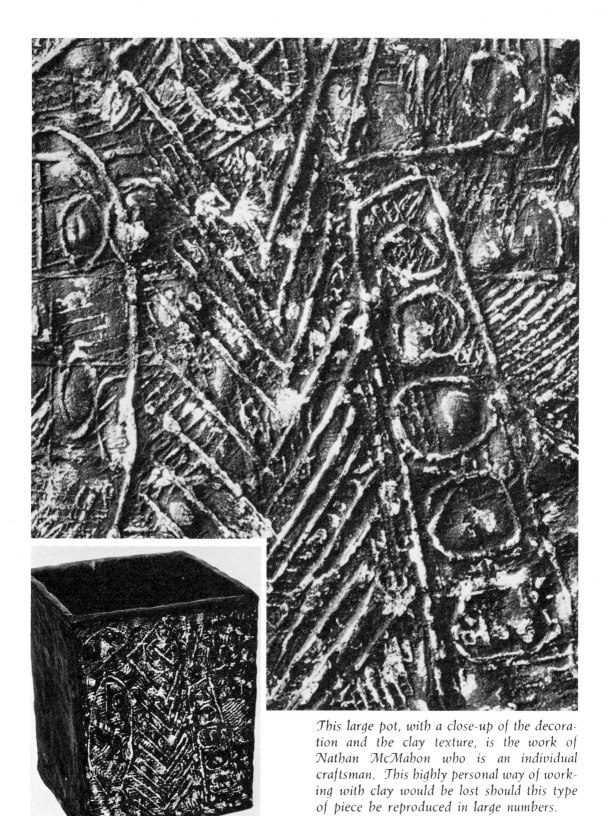

This large pot, with a close-up of the decoration and the clay texture, is the work of Nathan McMahon who is an individual craftsman. This highly personal way of working with clay would be lost should this type of piece be reproduced in large numbers.

IV HANDS AND CLAY

That faculty of beholding at a hint the face of his desire and the shape of his dream, without which the earth would know no lover and no adventurer.

JOSEPH CONRAD[1]

Hands as Tools

Of all the tools that man has devised for working with clay, the excellence and dexterity of the hand as a tool are beyond comparison. Hands which are controlled and manipulated through the mind and the emotional responses are the tools of one's thoughts. When clay, man's hands, and man's imagination work together, man's thoughts are communicated clearly and beyond verbal expression.

Using the hand as the basic tool should be the first experience: the student learns what the clay will do as his hands pinch, poke, push, twist, and turn it. Next he may search for the many ways his hands

[1] *Lord Jim*, chap. 16.

can be used, discovering perhaps that no two people will twist, pull, or poke in exactly the same way. There is no longer a separation between what his hands do and how the material reacts, how far it will bend, what its supporting strength is, why it cracks, and why it doesn't crack.

The hands, as tools, manipulate, control, and guide the clay.

Hands are used consciously and unconsciously in many ways.

Hands are used as tools to poke, squeeze, and shape the clay.

The clay has been pressed into a slab by hand and divided into four areas.

The thumb and forefinger pinch and push the clay in the first area. The hands will be used in other ways to make different designs in each area.

Exploration of Material

The limitations of the material cannot really be taught. Like the possibilities of the material, they must come from personal experience through actual handling. The rewarding fact, however, is that the teacher will become aware of the extent of ingenuity within each student while he explores materials in this way. The teacher must understand how each student works and recognize the results of the way in which he works. These are his identification marks, his style, his way of solving his problem. Not only must these be sought and found, they must be fed, understood, and respected.

Marguerite Wildenhain states that "a way to discover how hands work may be this: take a slab of clay, either pressed by hand or rolled with a rolling pin, and divide it roughly into large and small areas. By using the fingers, knuckles, and palms, bend, pinch, push, and twist each area differently."[2] The experience will be a combined visual, tactile and textural discovery. The individual student will become aware of how his hands are working.

Another way is to take a fat coil of a fair length and, by bending and twisting it vertically and horizontally, make it into a form without destroying the coil as a whole piece. The significant point here is that one should not destroy the nature of the clay as it twists and turns.

[2] Method used by Marguerite Wildenhain, Pond Farm, Guerneville, California.

Wedging Clay

Clay must be in good condition before it is used, that is, it must be of the same consistency or texture throughout. It must be plastic or wet enough so that it will stay together, retaining a certain shape after it has been formed. Clay should not be so dry that it crumbles when it is formed. Neither can it be so

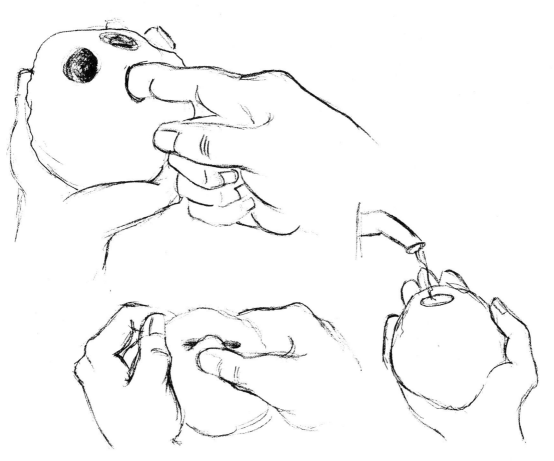

To add water to clay if it becomes too dry, poke holes in the clay ball. With a sponge or in some other way fill the holes with water and seal it inside the lump. Then slowly and carefully work the ball. Some of the water will squeeze out but the rest can be worked in quite easily. Continue to wedge the ball until it is consistent in texture.

wet that it sticks to the hands, making it hard to shape; nor can it contain lumps of dry clay mixed in with the wet. If it is too dry, water can be added by poking a finger into the center of the ball of clay and filling the hole with water. This helps to distribute the water more evenly when the clay is worked. If the clay is too wet, it must be spread on a piece of plaster or wood, which will draw off the excess water. If the clay contains dry lumps, these must be broken and blended into the wet clay. Then before it is used it must be "wedged" into a ball or loaf of the desired even texture for working. Large quantities of clay must be wedged for small children by the teacher, as it requires considerable strength in the hands and arms.

Wedging is often referred to as kneading or mixing materials to a desired consistency. In the classroom, hand wedging is a simple method which can be used to great advantage, for it teaches the beginner a great deal about the feel of clay as well as assuring that the mixture is an even mix. A double handful of clay is made into a ball (as it is wedged, it will become smaller and be a good handful). The ball is passed, with some force, from one hand to the other in a sharp rhythmical motion. The hands are about four inches apart. Each hand, in a squeezing motion, puts pressure on the ball but never enough to deform the shape of the ball. To insure good wedging, this should be done about fifteen times. It should be remembered that making a coil or rolling clay with a pin is, in a sense, wedging, too.

The act of wedging is difficult to explain in words and equally difficult to explain in picture form. In hand wedging, the ball shape is retained. However, the rhythmic motion with force destroys the air bubbles, and the clay becomes even in texture.

The Pinch Pot

When small children are first given clay, their natural reaction to its plasticity is to squeeze or punch it. In fact, this is a very natural reaction for most people. When it is discovered that pushing will make a hole, the clay, in many instances, becomes a vessel. There are many experiences which can be related to this first reaction, such as the animal or figure squeezed or pulled from one lump of clay or the very primitive method of making a bowl, the pinch pot. A pinch pot is easily made by taking a ball of clay, which is rounded by rolling between the hands, and pressing the thumb into the middle of the ball. As it is pinched between the thumb and fingers, the pot grows in size and form. The size, character, and treatment is determined by the student.

After the clay has been rounded into a ball, the thumb or a finger is gently pressed into the middle of the ball.

The clay is securely supported by the palm of one hand. As the clay is pinched between the thumb and the finger, it is turned in a slow rhythmical motion. As it turns, the pot grows in size and form.

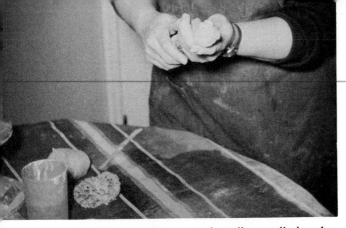

To begin making a coil, pull or roll the clay between the hands to make an oblong form. A piece of canvas is used to protect the table, as well as to provide a suitable surface to work on. Clay will not stick to the canvas.

The clay is rolled with a slight, even pressure from the palms to the finger tips. To keep the coil an even thickness as it gets longer, spread the fingers to cover a large area. If a very large coil is necessary, on the forward motion roll or move the hands from the center outward to the tips of the coil, and return to the center of the coil on the backward roll.

Coiling

Children usually refer to "making snakes out of clay" when they speak about the coiling process. That is the easiest way to explain coiling, which is done simply by rolling the clay between the palms or on a board or table top with the palms. A slight pressure from the palms will make the clay extend while it is being rolled. The building of coils is usually done in circular fashion by starting as a spiral (or by starting with a slab base) and building one coil on top of the other until the form desired is reached. This is the traditional manner of building primitive ware.

Some people use the palm or the whole hand in coiling, seldom using the fingers.

When coiling a pot, it is often more reliable if the pot is begun on a base that is made of a flat slab of clay or clay formed over a hump. If the coils are not joined perfectly when used for the base, they have a tendency to pull apart in the fire.

If the clay is not moist or "tackie" enough to join the coils together well, take a sharp tool and crosshatch fine lines where the next coil is to be added. This crosshatching, or scratching, is called scoring.

Next mix clay and water to the consistency of light cream slip and paint this over the crosshatching.

37

Add the coil, holding it carefully and with little pressure so that it will not break. Coils may be added just the length of the circumference of the bowl or by continual winding until the coil has all been used. Ends may be overlapped, being pinched firmly together, or they may meet tip to tip. The ends must be firmly joined with adequate pressure.

Coils may be smoothed, Indian fashion, so that the coil making process is no longer visible, or they may be joined as in this case, leaving the coil visible. This creates a natural and visible structural decoration.

A rim is added. It is made of a coil which has been pinched to the shape desired. Because this is not a mechanical process, the unevenness of the shape must be expected. It is the individual beauty of this kind of ware.

38

Slab Building

A knife or some tool for cutting, a rolling pin, and a piece of canvas or burlap are necessary for making slab pieces. The clay is rolled out flat on the cloth, and pieces are cut from the rolled slab. A slab piece has various sections which are fitted together to form the whole object. Individual preference decides the thickness of the clay, how the sections are to be joined, and whether the clay is left to harden or is put together in a wet state. If the clay is used wet, the object is put together immediately after the rolling and cutting. Should the student wish to wait, placing the slabs on a piece of plaster will help. The plaster will draw the moisture from the clay at a speed that depends on dryness of the plaster. The slabs are then used when the clay is firm enough to be handled, yet not dry enough to prevent good joining.

Joining

The method of joining used should be appropriate to the way of forming and the building processes the student uses naturally. It will eventually become a very natural way of working for the individual and will become a part of the form indistinguishable from the whole. Joining should not be artificial looking, but should show the character of the method used.

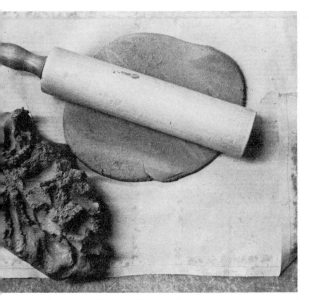

Clay is rolled with a rolling pin on a piece of canvas.

The clay is cut to the desired shape with a knife. This shape will be the wall of the pot.

The slab is decorated. This is one method, by using clay stamps. Hands also make excellent tools for decorating.

A slab for the base is rolled on canvas and placed on a piece of plaster. The wall is picked up gently and shaped, placing the two edges exactly together.

With one hand, support the inside wall where the two edges come together. With the other hand, gently join the two edges. Should the two edges not join well, score them, apply slip, and add a coil.

With a tool, cut the excess clay away from the base of the pot leaving about ½ inch extending beyond the base. Then with the finger, pull the excess inward and upward to seal the base edge. Again, support the wall from the inside with one hand while pressing with the other.

Add a rim by making a coil and shaping it to the desired form.

The finished pot. The clay has been used wet and has not been allowed to dry except for the base which was put on plaster. The plaster block is used for building so that the piece can be easily moved to the drying area. When moving it, handle it carefully and gently. Any pressure will deform the shape.

For the small child the clay should be plastic and the consistency for workability; that is, it should be soft enough to be easily joined without using slips, coils, and scoring. Making animals, figures, or some form which needs to be put together in sections is good experience. Teach the child that, when two sections are joined, pushing together and giving each piece a slight twist will assure the joint. Fingers then can be used to give the added security by smoothing the clay where the two sections come together.

As experience grows, students can use all methods of joining: hands, slip, and coils. Scoring, slips, and coils are usually needed when the clay has become somewhat hardened; to add a wet piece of clay to a dried area would cause cracking. A tool is used to score (scratch) the surface of the two areas to be joined, and slip is painted on the two sides. A coil is placed between the two areas, and the pieces are then pushed together. Under pressure the soft coil will squeeze beyond the joint and adhering to the slip, which has dampened the scored surface. The coil excess is then smoothed off in a natural way.

Fingers can also be used for joining, especially in the coil process. The way the hands or fingers are used will determine the character and the texture of the finished form. The ways in which the hands can be used in joining coils are

When joining two sections of clay, push them together hard and give them a good twist. Then take the finger and smooth the two areas together to secure the joint. Both lumps of clay should be of the same softness. Clay which is too firm to twist in the hands without breaking will not blend and join firmly.

The clay is scored with a sharp tool where two areas are to be joined. The scoring, or scratching, digs up the surface of the clay so that the slip and the "tackie," or soft coil, will join easily together.

Slip is painted on the scored area.

The coil is added.

almost without number; it is an exciting exploratory experience for individuals or a group of students to discover how many they can invent.[3] This can be done with small test pieces, as suggested previously.

Students should be made aware that there are a few technical hazards in working with clay; the important ones are air pockets, improper drying, and poor joinings. An air pocket is a hole surrounded by a solid mass of clay; it is not dangerous unless the piece is not thoroughly dry. The heat of the kiln will cause the moisture in the piece to become steam, which will create pressure within the air pocket and cause an explosion that will endanger all the ware in the kiln. Consequently, pieces must be thoroughly dry before they are put into the kiln. Touching a piece to the cheek is a good test, for it will feel damp if it is not completely dry. Poor joining can be a hindrance and become distressing, because it will cause cracks or complete separation of areas while the piece is drying or is in the fire. It should be emphasized that it is difficult and usually impossible to repair any of these accidents, although here the lesson must often be taught through experience.

[3] Ibid.

It is an exciting exploratory experience to find how many ways coils can be joined. These are small test pieces which can be used to make or to decorate real pieces of pottery or sculpture.

The walls are added. The coil shows at the corner between the two walls and between the base and the walls.

By pushing the walls with a slight pressure, the coils will squeeze beyond the joint. The way the finger or hand is used will determine the character and texture of the finished joint. It may even become a decorative detail on the finished piece.

V | FORM, ORDER, AND IMAGINATION

Pebbles show nature's way of working stone. . . . The mystery of the hole — the mysterious fascination of caves in hillsides and cliffs.

HENRY MOORE[1]

Design and the Forming Process

Design is so deeply imbedded in the forming process that it cannot and should not be considered a thing to be taught separately or prior to the actual experience with the material. While the teacher is encouraging him to learn the natural way the clay works and to discover his own ways of working with it, the student will become increasingly critical of the things he has formed. He will question, perhaps not in art vocabulary or in terms of the principles of design, but in very

[1] "Notes on Sculpture," in Myfanwy Evans's *The Painter's Object*, edited by Brewster Ghiselin (Berkeley: University of California Press, 1952), p. 75.

Pebbles show nature's way of working.

Caves are fascinating and mysterious.

practical terms related to the particular object which he is making. The teacher may be able to show him the way to better design by questions such as, How does it feel in your hand? Does the form hold together? Are all the parts the same size, or should they vary? Does it look and feel like clay or is it more like wood or some other material? Is it strong or weak looking?

The haunting factor in any kind of guidance at this formative stage is the decision the teacher must make: whether to tell the student what he might do or to leave him alone to search for a solution himself. To set up specific problems in line, proportion, emphasis, etc., seems to defeat the main purpose of both the teacher and the student. That purpose is to make an object which is unified and consistent in its whole appearance and its construction. Good design is both reasoning and intuition; therefore, the actual teaching of it can be meaningful only as it is related to use and sensed through the act of forming and giving substance to a concept. Each solution will bear indelibly the mark of the person who made it.

Ways of Showing Design

An effective way of pointing up good structural design is to show colored slides and photographs of nature forms which the student can relate to the design problems as they arise in his work. At times it may be even more effective to allow the student to search for the meaning of nature forms himself without discussing them. In any event, visual material of this kind should be presented in such a way that the student will not feel that he must copy from it directly. Nature has much to offer him in knowledge of structure, but when he attempts to represent nature directly, the experience can be as much of a hindrance as that of copying from another person's work. The student's own interpretative drawings (not rigidly copied) from nature itself will help make him more conscious of form and growth. But when he attempts, for example, to make a dish that looks exactly like a leaf, the nature of clay as a plastic material is destroyed. The result is neither a good leaf nor a good dish. Nor does imagination grow from this type of experience.

An infinite variety of pendant forms on one vine. (Gourds)

Texture accents the living form rather than contradicting it. (Cat in tree)

A wintering plant encloses and protects its growing center. (Mullen)

A summer plant opens and spreads. (Mt. Laurel)

*A sequence of forms from sphere to crescent.
(Bowl with fruit and nuts)*

*Geometric forms reveal the internal structure
of the earth. (Crystal forms)*

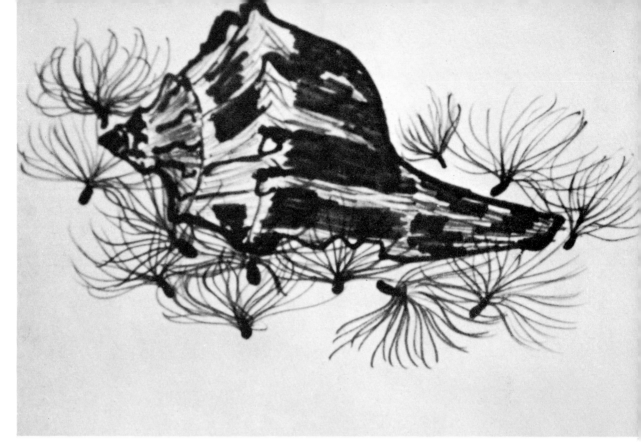

Student drawing of a growing plant — Linden Hall Junior College. (Felt-tip pen and ink drawing)

Student drawing of a shell and milkweed seeds — Linden Hall Academy. (Felt-tip pen and ink drawing)

Student drawing of gourds — Linden Hall Academy. (Felt-tip pen and ink drawing)

Nature and Design

One must resort to nature's laws of growth to understand fully both design and decoration. "In nature and in man's art the process of making and growth bring apparently unrelated elements into unity, and something whole is created. The laws of form and forming exist in nature as well as in man's art. The processes used are, in turn, revealed in that which is created."[2] As an example, the tree in nature grows as one. It is not born as a full-grown tree, yet the pulp, the bark, the leaves, and the color have a way

[2] Charles Harder, Chairman, Department of Design, Alfred University, comments to a class in ceramics.

of growing *as one* from the seed to the first shoot to the full grown tree. These are all closely related parts without which the form of the tree could not exist. But when man makes an object, he must do so in steps, building the steps gradually into a whole. When working with clay he first makes the form, afterward adds the slip, and later the glaze, and finally fires his product. It is only after all these steps have been taken that the object is recognized and understood to be the completed expression of the individual. Often this step-by-step process misleads the individual and prevents him from being able to follow completely the laws of growth in nature.

"It must be remembered that man himself is a part of nature and some of the features of his 'making' or 'art' resemble the results of nature's 'laws of growth.' As man experiments, his way is guided by his reason, intuition, intention, impulse, imagination, and emotion. Nature also experiments (man is an example) although her trials and errors can be read only in time and through evolution. But, in detail, nature also follows intrinsic plans and patterns of growth and regeneration which are similar to man's way of 'making.' Man's art reveals the way of his reason, the strength of his purpose, the intensity of his imagination and all of his unique 'humanness.' In each case the process of growth is evident in the final result."[3]

3 *Ibid.*

In hand building, decoration is part of the forming process, which grows from the individual's approach and his use of the materials. What is done during the process of forming may be sufficient decoration in itself. If added decoration is used, its purpose may be to emphasize the form or to enhance it. Sensitivity to the character of the material and the effect of simple tools is important in gaining an understanding of *when* or *when not* to add decoration. The big question will always be, "Does the form have enough to say by itself, or must something be added to make the statement more clear?" The question can be answered only by the individual. Teachers may suggest, but the final statement remains the student's expression.

Decoration, then, is the material itself, the process of building, and the surface enrichment, which, as a whole, in turn, reveals the maker. The material itself may be decoration in a sense; then the beholder will know that the object has been made with clay. The construction of

The coils are left showing that the pot has been made of coils. The rim is also a coil which has been pinched to give it variation and to show that this is the end of the pot as the foot is the beginning — Linden Hall Academy.

the form is structural decoration, showing how the material has been used in the forming process, whether it has been made with coils or slabs, for example. Texture and color may be inherent parts of the material, or they may be surface treatments. "Surface treatment" means that which is done after the basic form has been completed. Some examples are the adding of slips, glazes, and carving. Decoration, therefore, helps one to recognize and understand the objects which he sees and feels; this should be a natural part of the total design. Italo de Francesco states it this way:[4] First among the concepts that underlie good design in the crafts is the relation of form to material. The qualities of each material should be exploited to the utmost. Meantime, no medium should be forced beyond its inherent possibilities. . . . It is a mark of good craftsmanship to employ only those decorative treatments that become one with the material rather than an ornament for its surface. . . . Utilizing the textural possibilities of a surface may relieve monotony without altering form, the character of the material, or the object. The current mode of doing more with the material itself than with surface decoration is an endeavor to retain the integrity of the material.

[4] *Art Education — Its Means and Ends* (New York: Harper & Bros., 1958), p. 455.

A piece of scrap wood is used to help assure the joint. Notice that one hand always supports the coils from the inside. When using a tool, several layers of coils may be added before the joining is done. This texture becomes a surface treatment.

Kinds of Decoration

The student should have some idea, gained by experience, of what the materials will do in the plastic state and what happens to them after they have been fired. This may not be essential in the elementary grades, but it can and should be acquired by junior and senior high school students.

By way of introduction to clay, students may make hand-sized cookie shapes, freely patted, with textures made by pushing, scratching, poking, etc. Next they may apply slips, glazes, or both in various ways to the surface, and then fire the pieces. In this way they feel and see what has happened to the materials, how the glaze feels and what happens when it runs into the cracks, what happens to the color of the clay, the changes in glaze and slips, and what happens when glazes are applied over slips. Further experiments, with added knowledge, may now be made with simple yet beautiful wall plaques, pottery, and sculpture. Made larger and with a better understanding of materials and design, these first tests will be beautiful, and useful, too.

Hand-sized cookie shapes of one texture are made by pushing and poking the clay.

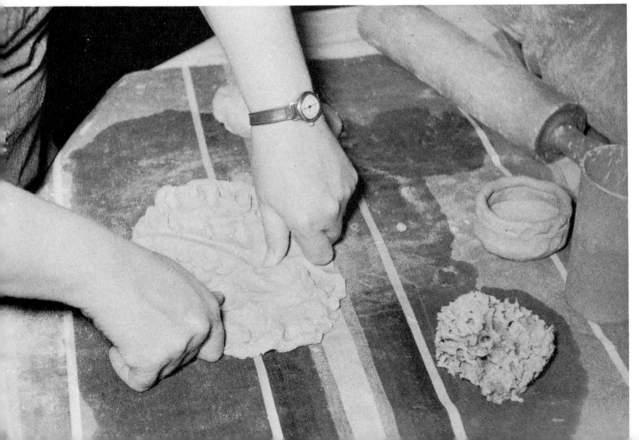

Hand Textures and Tool Textures

Previously, hand textures have been discussed in relation to the joining process. It must be remembered that this is decoration, too. Hand textures can also be used in slab building; after rolling and cutting, the slabs are decorated with the hands.

A slab piece decorated with hand textures.

61

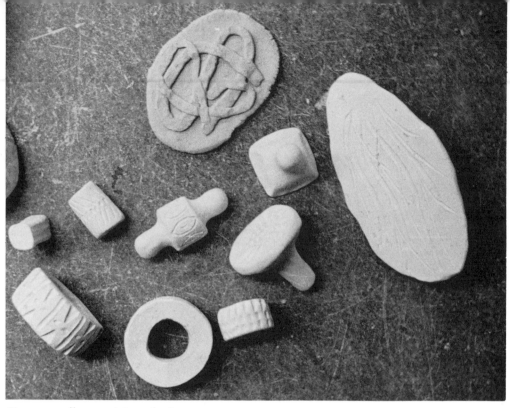

Clay stamps. Form small quantities of clay into shapes which will press into or roll on the clay. Do not make them too thick if they are to be fired. They may be used bone dry (unfired) or fired. Designs may be excised, incised and so forth, depending on the effect wanted.

A slab pot decorated with clay stamps.

Surface Treatment

Balls, coils, or slab pieces of some sort can be added to the surface, but they must look and feel as though they belong to the form. Usually they are added by first scoring the surface and then using a slip to ensure the joint.

While the clay is leather-hard, a stick, nail, or some other tool can be made to use as a stamp to vary the surface treatment. Other possibilities are to incise a line or carve the clay away, leaving a raised line.

Tools, other than the hands, can be used in the same way; they may be applied to the coiling process, slabs, or pinch pots.

Old spoons can be used for polishing the surface of the clay by applying the underside of the spoon bowl to the clay with reasonable pressure when it is in a leather-hard condition. This will make a shiny surface that will be retained after the firing. The Indians still use this method, but with stones instead of a spoon. The stones, from generations of potters using them constantly, have a high-polish texture that is similar to the bowl of a spoon.

There are other ways to use materials and tools for decorating. Many of the ways suggested can be used in combination to create interesting effects, but that must be done with organization and thought. If it is not, the result will be a confusion of textures which are unrelated to each other.

Polishing the clay surface with a spoon bowl. For best results the clay should be "leather-hard," that is, it should be firm but have some moisture in it. Pressure from the spoon causes the moisture and very fine particles of clay to rise to the surface; the combination of the two creates the gloss, which will remain even after firing.

Glaze as Decoration

Many times glaze is an adult concept which is forced on students, whose basic association with glaze has been with dinnerware. Students feel that glaze is the only acceptable way to finish a piece of pottery or sculpture. Here, again, it is important to explain the function of glaze in a simple, understandable way. The glaze is used as a covering, either for decorative purposes or to make a vessel tight or impervious to liquids. There are many objects, such as planters and sculpture, on which glazes do not have to be used. When the student understands the use of glaze, he should be free to decide whether he wants to use it or not.

Glaze should be dipped or poured on; painting is not a satisfactory way to apply it, because it is often unsuccessful. The proper methods may seem awkward at first, but after the student finds his way of working and develops a few skills he will discover different ways to use glaze.

Overlapping, or making glaze heavier in one area than on another, will cause one effect, while wiping off glaze in certain areas will create another. Either can be done with a sponge. Hot paraffin or liquid wax applied to parts of the piece by either painting or dipping will prevent glaze from sticking to the coated areas. This works particularly well; however, caution must be taken when using hot wax so that students will not burn themselves.

The need for using stilts in firing can be eliminated by waxing the foot of object to be glazed. This is necessary only in the glaze fire. Heat a pan of paraffin and dip the foot of the pot, or the base, into the melted paraffin. It needs to be held in the wax only a few seconds. The paraffin may also be painted on the base, but it must be done quickly. Once brushes are used for wax, they will not be usable for other types of painting.

First immerse the piece to be glazed in water. When this is done, the piece will take on a more even coat of glaze. The dipping must be done very quickly. If the piece is in the water any length of time, the glaze will not stick and the piece will have to be dried. The dipping cannot be done after any area has been glazed; it must precede all glazing.

Remember all glazing is done after the bisque fire. To glaze the inside of a pot, use either a pitcher or a cupful of glaze. Pour the glaze quickly into the pot and as soon as the pot is full pour the glaze out. When glazing, use buckets or dishpans so that there is plenty of glaze, and the student has elbow room for working.

There are two methods for glazing the outside of a pot. This one is called "pouring." Again use a pitcher or a cup to hold the glaze. Sticks can be laid across the glaze bucket so the pot can stand upside down over the bucket. In this way the glaze that runs off the pot runs back into the bucket. Pour the glaze quickly around the object to be glazed. The outside of the piece must be glazed at the same time as the inside for best results. Always do the inside of the piece first, so that it can be handled freely.

The second method is dipping. The pot is grasped at the base or at the rim and is pushed into the glaze quickly and pulled out quickly. If this is done slowly, the coating of glaze will be too heavy.

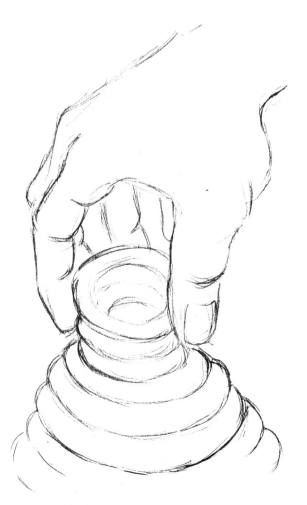

One way to hold the foot of a pot for dip glazing is shown.

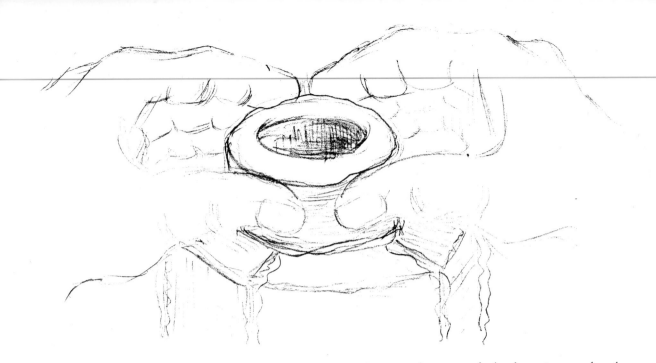

Some students may feel safer using two hands. Allow students to find their own way of holding things. They will feel more secure while working and achieve the same good results.

If some of the clay body is to show through the glaze after the piece has been "dipped" or "poured," a partially wet sponge will remove glaze from raised surfaces. Glazes can also be applied to small areas with a brush or with a sponge. It is not advisable to paint glaze on a whole piece for an uneven texture will result. It will not always stick to the area where glaze is wanted.

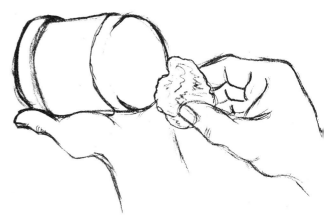

Take a damp sponge and carefully clean off the areas that have been waxed. Handle the pot lightly but firmly enough so the pot will not slip. The hands should be completely dry to prevent marring the glaze applied on the surface.

Use of Slips

Slips can be used in many ways; they can be painted on with a brush, scratched through, dipped on, or sponged on or off. Other ways can be found by experiment. Slips can be used under glazes or by themselves.

If the student is stimulated to find his way and if he is taught to work without hesitation and is given assurance, he will discover that ideas will flow easily and constantly while he works with these materials and tools.

The clay is red and the slip is white. The slip has been used only as an accent for the line of the coat, the hat, and the basket. The pot has no slip decoration — Linden Hall Junior College.

VI LEARNING WITH CLAY

The precious porcelain of human clay.

LORD BYRON[1]

A Good Environment

The teacher, without too much difficulty, can supply the environment which will further the development of the tactile and visual senses. The good teacher will ensure that students will have every possible association with nature. Studying the formation of the earth's structure and the origin of clay creates a firm understanding of the material which they are using for creative work. Nature's forms can be brought to the classroom by students and the teacher. While studying the patterns of growth in nature, students can actually be studying design. Bark from trees shows texture; stones can be studied for a variety of shapes, sizes, and colors; dried grasses and weeds will interest students in texture, color, and

[1] *Don Juan*, Canto IV, Stanza 11.

construction of form. Insects, as well as many other objects, when seen under a simple magnifying glass or a microscope have interesting variations in design. House plants growing in the classroom or the planting of some flowers or weeds will increase student understanding of nature. Field trips, not only to woods but to natural-history museums where animals and other nature forms can be studied carefully, will help immensely to further student experiences. A visit to the zoo should be considered. Whenever the actual experience can not be had, visual aids such as slides or film strips should be used. Visual aids can also supplement the field trip by reviving the actual experience in detail.

Study the formation of the earth's structure.

Bark from trees shows texture.

A variety of textures, colors, and forms are found in nature.

Films which show the industrial processes are available. Students, especially in the junior and senior high school, should be told the part that the commercial pottery industry plays in our society. Examples of commercial products should be brought to the classroom to be handled and carefully studied. This is also an effective way to create better student understanding of what he is doing; it contrasts the way he is working as an individual craftsman with the factory processes.

A pot has been coiled by a student. A living plant was selected by the student and planted in the pot — Linden Hall Academy.

The history of pottery should not be overlooked. Seeing how people have made vessels and sculpture from clay to fit their own needs (association, in some way) will make the student's own experiences more meaningful. Whenever possible, museum trips should be arranged. Good examples of work in clay and in other materials, originals or reproductions, can be brought to the classroom. Here again, slides, strip films, or films can be used effectively. The history of pottery should be studied for the sociological aspects rather than for the study of design as such, although design should be pointed out in relation to the process of making and the purpose for which the object was made. The purpose of museum visits and material should obviously never be to attempt to reproduce the object the students may see.

These suggestions are, of course, dependent on the age and the advancement of the student. The wise teacher will know which of the many enriching experiences mentioned will be most worthwhile for a particular class.

Jar from graveyard — East Hampton, Long Island, New York.

Pottery stamps — Jaynda, West Coast, Puerto Rico.

Pottery bowl — Virginia.

Jar — Guatemala.

Pottery heads — Salvador.

Pottery figures — Venezuela.

78

Owl pot — E. Jackson, Potter, Cherokee, North Carolina.

Bean pot — Virginia Romero, Potter, Taos Pueblo, New Mexico. Mrs. Romero is one of the last Indian potters to make vessels for daily use.

Bowl — Juan, Potter, Santa Clara Pueblo, New Mexico. Bird — Potter, Marie Z. Chino, Acoma Pueblo, New Mexico.

Basic Factor To Be Taught

Within all the areas of hand-built pottery there are many ways to be explored. The ideas presented in this book are only suggestions which should lead teachers and students on to new discoveries. To accomplish this with confidence there are basic procedures which the teacher may have to demonstrate, and it is important that he will have had some previous experience with clay. He should be able to coil, do a pinch pot, and build with slabs, because in many instances when the student has had no previous experience, he will have to be shown. How to make joints, as well as how to glaze and the other mechanical factors, are a part of teaching.

True Role of the Teacher

At best teachers can do more than present materials and whatever they know of their use. They often fail to make clear to their students that they are hoping for more than techniques. They fail because they do not wish to interfere with personal expression or create self-consciousness in their students which will disturb the spontaneous response so necessary in creative work. Too, teachers find it difficult to define for students the intangible word "creativeness." Even teachers may never fully understand the fusion that happens through the creative process, that which occurs when the individual, his imagination, and his materials work together. Yet the teacher can build within each student the confidence to find his own way of working with materials and do work which is worthy of his ability. For a teacher this is the major part of the task, the way through which the individual's potential is discovered. Words of confidence in a student's work are often far more effective and necessary than specific suggestions.

Goal for Teacher and Student

It is not impossible to explain to students that their own work is the most important thing and that, because each person in the class is different, each piece of work will be, or should be, different. This will not only help the student but should be the goal of the teacher. If the students are allowed to find their own way, then the teacher, without difficulty, will soon be able to recognize each student's product in a group of work.

Importance of Student Freedom

There is a delicate balance which must be struck between how much a teacher should do for students and how little. What may work for one student or group may not work for another. Educational theories and ideas and even teacher decisions may sound contradictory if the teacher is not fully aware of his true function. Dr. Daniel Prescott makes this statement:[2]

[2] Daniel Alfred Prescott, *Emotion and the Educative Process* (Washington, D.C.: American Council on Education, 1938), p. 103.

Student work — Toledo Museum of Art School. Children's Saturday classes.

Two groupings of individual student work. Note the difference in handling of coils in the pottery and the different approaches and subject matter in the sculpture — Linden Hall Academy.

"The way to maturity of aesthetic appreciation possibly lies through the widest experience, under guidance if possible, but better under conditions of complete freedom than under regimentation. The latter acts quickly and effectively to stifle appreciation."

He continues in another chapter to say:[3]

"Unfortunately experience overweighted with failure 'proves' to many children that they are 'no good' — even though they actually possess adequate intelligence and energy. Either too much success or too much failure may warp a person's judgement of his proper role in life."[3] In a book published in 1892, Ellen Stephen Hildreth expresses it this way:[4]

"The very natural desire of the teacher to have something to show for the time spent must be put aside and the child let absolutely alone while busy with the clay. The child that does not actively work at the clay will require some attention, and if disorderly, will require even more."

Exploration

The beginning stages of exploration are always difficult for the student as well as for the teacher. Students must be encouraged continually so that confidence develops from within. Only when the student reaches an impassé in his individual problem should the teacher discuss design. Even then, suggestions can not be obligatory.

[3] *Ibid.*, p. 124.

[4] *Clay Modeling in the Classroom* (Springfield, Mass.: Milton Bradley Co., 1892), p. 16.

A teacher who continually feels the necessity to help the student with his work by constructing a bit of wall, coiling a few layers, or specifically stating how a form should be ("to show how") is automatically leaving his identity within the student's piece. If something needs to be demonstrated by the teacher, it can be done on the side, on something personal that the teacher has prepared for the purpose. If the teacher is capable and it seems profitable as far as inspiring students is concerned, he may find moments when he may work along with his students on a piece of his own. Young people often wonder whether the teacher is able to do the work which he so willingly assigns to them.

A Difficult Lesson

"Hand-sitting" is one of the biggest and most difficult lessons a teacher must learn. Unless he has absorbed this lesson and believes in it, he can defeat the whole purpose behind creativity in art education. During the period of developing skills and learning materials, the student is also struggling to reveal his identity. True and complete identity does not come during this period, but it is emerging and can be observed. Therefore, it is during this time especially that the student must be left alone.

Understanding the Student

Teaching is never easy, whether the teacher is a beginner or a master. Not only must he understand the student as well as possible, he must understand himself; for he is teaching not only procedures but a method and way of life. He must be alert to the student who desires to talk about himself through his work, and he must also be understanding of another student who believes his work is speaking for him and is complete within itself. Then again, he must sense when the student feels he has nothing to say within his work, or needs a period of rest, or needs to express himself freely in some other way, perhaps verbally. Unless the art teacher, a creative person himself, remembers that there are moments when he has exhausted the well, has used up the energy in some other direction, he will not realize that the same thing can happen to his students. He must be mindful of the people who need the assurance that what they are doing is acceptable; the teacher's approval will often change insecurity into confidence, stimulating the student to achieve what he wants and to overcome difficulties in his work.

Above all the teacher must realize the sad truth that there are a few students who will never be reached or touched by him. Fortunately, there are others whom he will never know he has reached; for the things which he has given may not be drawn upon until the student is beyond the teacher's direct influence. Immediate satisfaction may come to the teacher only through those students who show visible results, but if the teacher is wise, he will know that he can never be sure when and how the moment of touching occurs, and therefore he must continue to try to reach everyone.

VII EQUIPMENT, MATERIALS, AND HOUSEKEEPING

By economy and good management, — by a sparing use of ready money and by paying scarcely anybody, — people can manage, for a time at least, to make a great show with very little means.

WILLIAM MAKEPEACE THACKERAY[1]

Simple Equipment

These are a few suggestions which a teacher with great interest and little money might use to expand the tools and equipment in his department or classroom. Some things can be begged, others found in secondhand stores at little cost, and others gathered just by asking.

❧ *A wedging board* can be made by building a wood frame and filling it with plaster. The plaster should be three or four inches thick; the whole board should be raised from the table about an inch. The air space will help the plaster dry out while it is being used.

[1] Vanity Fair, vol. 2, chap. 2.

Simple equipment, such as rolling pins, gallon jars, cups, cans of various sizes for storing dry materials, rubber spatulas, or plate cleaners to clean pans as well as stir materials, can easily be collected.

Mixing plaster. To speed the preparation of working bats and wedging boards, there are a few simple rules to follow. To make the job easier measure the water and the plaster. Use ½ pint of water to 11 ounces of plaster, or for double quantity use 1 pint of water to 1 pound 6 ounces of plaster. Always add the plaster to the water (never add the water to the plaster), sifting it through the hands. Do not stir the mixture until all of the plaster has been sifted into the water. Then stir the plaster until the mixture thickens to a light cream consistency. To stir, slide the hand into the mixture and move it without breaking the surface, at the same time breaking up all lumps. Remove the hand carefully and immediately pour the mixture into the prepared forms. Tapping the sides of the frame will help remove bubbles created by pouring.

87

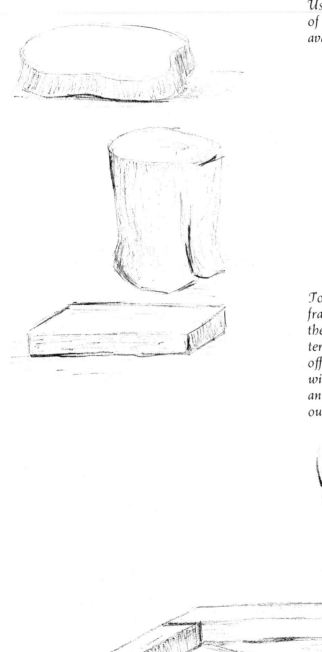

Use a tree trunk, cross-grain slab, or a plank of wood for a wedging board if plaster is not available.

To make a wedging board, construct a wood frame about 4 inches deep. Pour plaster into the frame completely filling it. Allow the plaster to harden, or set. Raise the wedging board off the table or other surface where is is used with blocks of wood or bricks. This provides an air space which allows the plaster to dry out after use.

A large tree trunk, or any good-sized piece of dry wood, also will work; neither requires any plaster, because the wood will absorb the moisture.

❧ *Plaster bats* for individual use can be made in paper plates or shoe-box lids. They save the desk tops from scratching, and clay will not stick to a bat as it does to cloth or paper. By means of bats, clay pieces may be moved easily without disturbing the work while it is still wet.

Plaster bats. Pour plaster into shoe box lids, paper plates, or any other paper boxes to make individual bats for each student to work on. To make enough bats for a class economically and efficiently mix large quantities of plaster in a bucket or a large bowl.

❀ *Hand sieves* (old flour sifters) can be used for mixing dry materials such as clay, glazes, and slips.

❀ *Plastic bags* and pieces of plastic may be used to store moist clay and cover individual pieces.

❀ *Rolling pins* or lengths of broom handles serve for rolling clay on *burlap*, *pieces of canvas* (old awnings), or *heavy muslin*. Canvas makes a good desk-top covering and working surface, although it is hard to remove pieces from the desk to drying areas when they are built up on canvas.

Hand sieves can be used for mixing dry materials. Old colanders will work too, particularly for clay. Sift materials through about five times to make sure they are well mixed.

Buckets for mixing glazes, sticks to stir as well as to use in glazing, sponges for cleaning tables and cleaning pottery after glazing, a pan, small stove, paraffin for waxing the bottom of pottery and sculpture are all readily available.

❖ *Jars*, the gallon size, will serve for storing mixed glazes and slips; smaller jars should be kept on hand for smaller quantities. School cafeterias, hospitals, and restaurants have these jars for the asking.

❖ *Cans*, the frozen-fruit-juice size, make good individual slip or water containers for desks. Coffee cans, shortening cans, etc. are best for storing dry materials.

❖ *Pails* with lids are necessary for storing clay. If plastic is available, wrap clay first; if not, cover the clay with wet burlap and keep it wet. Keep the lid on tightly when the pail is in use.

❖ *Tools*, excellent ones, can be made from tongue depressors, popsicle sticks, and wood discarded by the school's industrial arts shop. Let the student carve or sand the wood into the shape he desires.

Knives need not be bought. Old paring knives or old silverware or any tool which will cut will serve the purpose.

Spoons, forks, and conks, as well as wheels from toys, wire brushes, and so on, can be used for decorating.

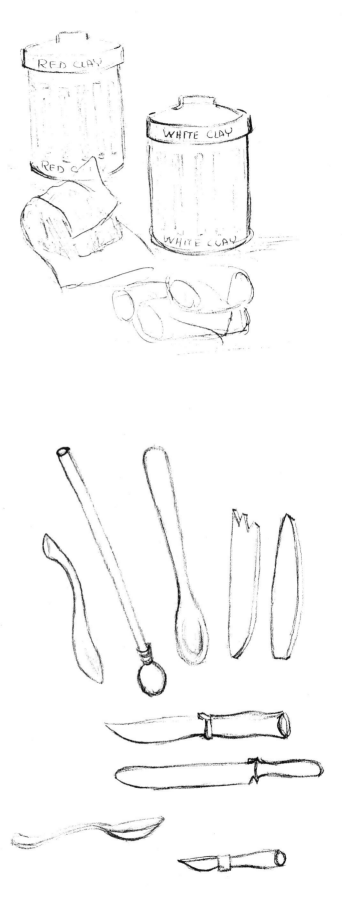

Wrap clay in plastic and then store it in cans with lids. Mark the lids and the bottoms of the cans with the color or kind of clay. This will help students put the right lids on the right cans. Clay can be wrapped in small or large bundles for storage.

All types of knives can be helpful. Spoons are used for polishing. Wood spoons with long handles may be used to support the inside of a pot where openings are too small for hands or fingers. A sponge tied onto a stick may serve the same purpose. Some tools can be made from tongue depressors or carved from scrap wood.

❧ *Heat lamps* can be used, but with great care; for they tend to cause cracking and warping. However, they may save time in the drying process. When pieces are put under the lamp to dry, they must be rotated every few minutes.

❧ A large *plaster drying bat* for freshly mixed clay can be made by lining a cardboard box with about two inches of plaster. Because the plaster expands in setting, the cardboard may break, but that will not destroy the form. Make the form about four or five inches deep and from twelve to eighteen inches in width and length. All measurements are inside dimensions of the finished bat. Any large flat surface of dry brick, stone, wood, or thick plaster will be useful for drying out large quantities of wet clay.

❧ If there is opportunity, dig native clay. Surface clays are close to the top soil and can often be found when house foundations are dug. Dry the clay and pulverize it by grinding and sifting through a screen, thus removing stones and sticks. Moisten the clay, wedge it, and use it. For those who wish to be more careful the clay may be watered to slip consistency and put through a fine-mesh screen. After it has been screened, pour the clay mixture into plaster box suggested above; excess water from the clay will be absorbed by the plaster. The dryer the plaster bat is, the less time it will take to absorb the moisture.

✤ When coiling, make a series of coils and put them between damp cheesecloth or some cloth. They will stay tacky and be ready for use.

Rotate pieces put under the heat lamp about every two or three minutes. Place the lamp about two or three feet away from the object to be dried.

Use a plaster box for drying very wet clay, or spread the clay thinly on a plank of wood or a plaster slab. Allow it to dry to the point where it can be wedged easily.

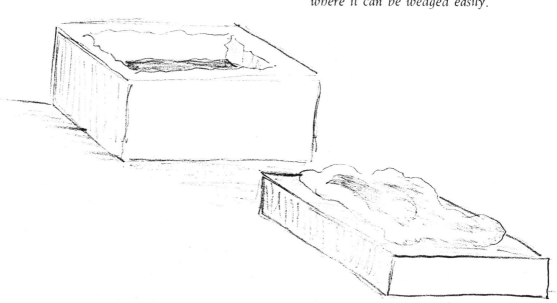

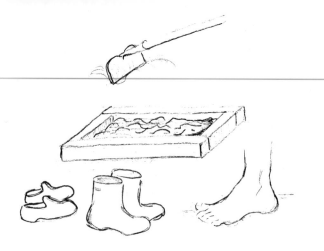

When mixing clay in a wood frame, the frame must be used on a cement or tile floor. Wedge with the bare feet, boots, rubbers, or old thick rubber-soled shoes. If this method seems undesirable, a hoe will help but wedging will have to be done by hand.

Use egg beaters to mix glazes or slips. Add the dry materials to the water and allow them to slake or settle before mixing with the beater. Use plastic bottles with narrow nozzles for decorating with slips.

❧ A wooden frame for mixing clay in large quantities is best built from 2 x 4's. Place the frame on a cement floor or other surface which can be cleaned and dried. Put a layer of clay in the form, add water, then more clay, more water, etc. Let the mixture set for about a day, then have students work it with bare feet by using body weight and treading.

❧ If the wood frame is not available for mixing dry clay, use a bucket or garbage can and the method of the next paragraph. Let the mixture set for several days or weeks, then hand-wedge.

❧ Egg beaters of the hand type are useful for mixing reasonably large quantities of glaze or slip. Mix in a bucket, a gallon jar, or a bowl.

❧ Discarded or secondhand restaurant-size potato and food mixers can be used for large quantities of clay or glaze.

❧ Plastic bottles with narrow nozzles can be used for decoration. Put thick slip into them and use as slip trailers.

Materials and Their Use

The teacher or student interested in finding detailed information on materials must resort to reference books on the subject. There are many available; they have been listed in the bibliography at the end of this book. It is more sensible and reasonable, if the teacher has little experience and very limited time, to buy prepared materials that are readily available from and pretested by commercial companies who supply schools and professional craftsmen.

Here, though, are a few suggestions which might aid the teacher who does have the time and wants to give his students themselves some experience in exploring materials.

❊ *Clay* can be bought in either a dry or moist state. For a year's work, it is estimated that about 175 pounds may be needed for twenty-five children. This is a very limiting amount and it will, of course, vary with the extensiveness of the program.

Most low-temperature clays are earth colors and fire to a red color. Clays which fire white at low temperatures are commercially prepared and contain other materials to control the firing range. When buying clays, order some of each which fire at the same temperature range, some moist and some dry. The dry can be used for preparing slips or experimenting with textures.

❊ To vary the *texture of the clay*, add 10 per cent grog, or ground walnut shells, rice hulls, or other finely ground organic matter. If the clay is the dry powder kind, sift the added material through the clay carefully. If the material is to be added to moist clay, the product must be wedged thoroughly and carefully. Roll clay flat with a rolling pin, sprinkle the grog, or other material on the clay, roll the two together, and wedge. Before it is actually used for building, be sure to test it. Mix only a small quantity (about a pound or less) of varying proportions of clay and other matter, make the product into cookie shapes, and fire.

❊ *Slips and engobes* are usually the same, although there is much confusion about the terms. The word "engobe" is French; and it always refers to a slip that is used for decoration. "Slip" means any clay in liquid state; a slip can be used for joining, for casting, and as a glaze, as well as for decorative purposes. For the classroom, we refer a liquid-clay mixture as slip, and it is used for a decorative purpose. It can be applied thin on raw, bone-dry, or bisque ware, and it can be dipped on or painted on, scratched through, or left as applied. When used thickly, it must be applied while the piece is wet or it will have a tendency to crack off the piece. Usually in the thick state it will leave a raised line when applied with a brush or a slip trailer. Also, test pieces should be made to see how it works. Slips can be made from clay whether moist or dry, but should be mixed carefully. The dry ingredients are added to the water and then left to slake for a short time. The amount of water used will determine the thinness or thickness of the slip.

❊ *Glazes* can be simplified by just buying several frit glazes. A frit glaze is one which has been prepared by previous firing to form a glass, after which it has been cooled and reground. By combining frits and adding as high as 10 per cent clay, the texture of the glaze can be changed from clear (transparent) to opaque. Colorants can be added to these mixtures to make colored glazes.

If this is too time-consuming, buy frit glazes that are transparent, opaque, or matt and vary them by using colored slips underneath.

❀ *Colorants* or stains are added to slips to change their color. Always work on a 100 per cent dry weight basis when adding coloring materials. For example, if red iron oxide is used, add 3 per cent of it to 100 per cent, or the total amount, of clay; that is, add 3 grams of red iron oxide for every 100 grams of clay. The amounts of colorants used are very small, and a half pound or a pound of a colorant will last quite a while.

❀ It is not necessary to buy a large variety of colorants for school purposes. The few listed should be enough; varying percentages will vary the color results. The amounts of colorants to be used have been tested; they should not be varied very much either way, because that would affect the glazes used over them.

Red iron oxide; use about 2 to 6 per cent.

Rutile; use 1 to 5 per cent.

Copper carbonate; use 2 to 5 per cent.

Stains:

Mason black; use 1 to 5 per cent.

Blue stain; use 1 to 2 per cent.

One-half pound or a pound of each will last for several years, depending on the extent of use. The stock will give a color range from red, blue, and yellow, to brown, depending on the colorants and amounts used. Combinations should be tried and then selected before making large quantities for classroom use. The percentages listed are the same for glazes or slips.

❧ *Dealers* who carry the equipment and supplies necessary for a clay program can be found listed in magazines such as *School Arts, Junior Arts & Activities, Craft Horizons,* and *The American Artist.* Those listed here are just a few suggestions.

American Art Clay Co., Indianapolis, Indiana; clay, glazes, tools, and kilns.

B. F. Drakenfeld & Co., Inc., 45-47 Park Place, New York 7; clay, glazes, tools, kilns, and kiln equipment and supplies.

Stewart Clay Co., 133 Mulberry Ave., New York; clay, glazes, frits, colorants, tools, kilns, and kiln equipment and supplies.

Pemco Corp., Baltimore, Maryland; frits, colorants and stains.

Ferro-Enamel Co., Cleveland, Ohio; frits, colorants, and stains.

Kilns and Firing

Companies which sell kilns will on request supply information concerning the process of firing and how to use the kiln for best results. There are many types of kilns, such as oil, gas, and electric, and there are variations in size and structure. Kilns have different firing temperatures and are usually classed as either high or low fire temperature. For school purposes the electric kiln may be the best. It is suggested that the temperature range of the kiln be carefully considered before buying. A high-temperature kiln will be more expensive, but its value lies in being able to use it (with time and experience) for experimentation in different temperature ranges. A low-fire kiln would be more limiting. Since a kiln is an expensive piece of equipment, it would seem best to purchase a type which would give as much range as possible and the greatest amount of service. Maybe the most important factor would be that the elements would be longer lasting and the danger of over-firing and harming or destroying elements would not be as severe. It is also suggested that size be considered; the actual firing box should have ample space to handle a good-sized group of student ware. Teachers can limit the size of students' work to a certain degree, but minute pieces are difficult to work on and, if he is to have a valid experience with clay, the student should have some choice in the size of his work without

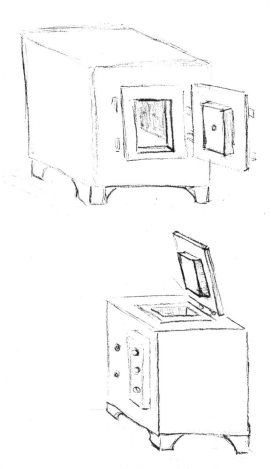

There are two types of electric kilns. One is a side-loading type in which the ware is loaded into the side of the kiln, the other is a top-loading type. Both types are good and which one is bought will depend on the buyer's preference and the space available for the kiln.

101

going to extremes. The author suggests a firing box of about 17 inches square or larger. That would hold on an average of twenty-five or thirty pieces, which would take care of many classroom groups.

❋ Locate the kiln where it will not be dangerous for the students. If it is in the classroom, in some way notify the students on the days when it is being fired.

❋ Before placing ware in the kiln, be sure it is dry. As mentioned previously, touch the piece to the cheek; if it feels cold, it is not dry. Check each piece carefully to see to the best of your ability that it will stand the fire.

❋ If there is still some doubt whether the pieces are not dry, "water soak" the kiln after it has been stacked. Leave the door open about two inches and also the peep hole and vents. Turn the kiln on at its lowest temperature for about two hours. Then close the door and peep hole and finish firing.

❋ When ordering clay, take note of its temperature or firing range and make sure that range coincides with the firing ranges of the kiln (if a low-temperature kiln is used). Also, make sure the glazes and frits used coincide with clay and kiln range.

❋ Cones are an important part of firing, for they tell when the desired temperature is reached. A cone is a small pyramid made of clay and glaze materials which will soften at a specific temperature. A number is stamped on the side of the cone which coincides with the specific temperature, such as:

$$c/05 = 1030° \, C — 1886° \, F$$
$$c/04 = 1050° \, C — 1922° \, F$$
$$c/03 = 1080° \, C — 1976° \, F$$

The cone is stamped as c/04 and not with the temperature. Cones are purchased from the dealers that carry kilns and clay supplies. Temperature charts will be supplied by the manufacturer upon request. The cones must coincide with the materials and the kiln; all of these things must work together for good results in firing. Even if a pyrometer or some other electrical gauge is used to read temperatures, it is always best to use cones too. The electrical temperature indicator may fail in the midst of a firing, but the cones will still continue to show when the desired temperature is reached.

If possible, it is best to set up cones so that there is some idea of what is happening in the kiln. For example, if the ware is fired to c/04, place cones c/05, c/04, and c/03 in the cone pack. The c/05 will tell when a temperature that is close to the desired temperature is reached, and that will be a warning to watch the kiln carefully. The c/04 cone will tell when the correct temperature has been reached, while the c/03 cone will show if the kiln has been overfired. The cones should be placed in such order that the lowest-temperature cone will fall first, the next temperature cone would follow, etc. Place the cone pack where it can be observed through the peep hole.

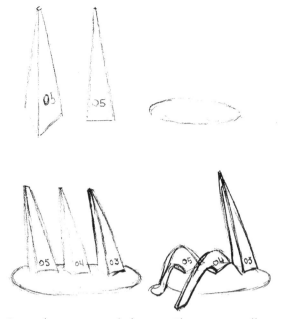

Cones have pyramid shapes. They are usually placed in a coil of clay with the cone numbers facing in the same direction. They have a slight tilt which shows the direction in which they will fall when melted if they are placed in the same direction that they tilt. This is an example of a possible cone pack for a cone 04 kiln. When the cones fall, the C/05 will melt the most, the C/04 has just gone over, while the C/03 remains standing.

Place the cones in the clay coil and push the coil together to give the cones protection. Break off excess clay. Take a small stick or toothpick and poke holes in the clay so the clay will dry out. This is important, for if the clay is wet when it is put into the kiln, it may explode like any other wet clay piece. Make the cone pack ahead of time so that the clay has a chance to dry.

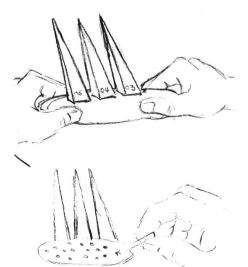

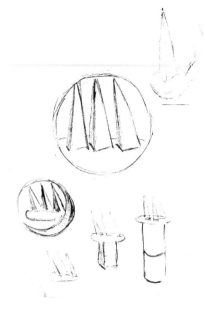

Place the cone pack where it can be easily seen through the peephole. If the cone pack cannot be seen when placed on the shelf, place it on one or more shelf supports until it can be seen. To make sure it can be seen after it is in place, stick a match in the clay, light it, and close the door. If it can't be seen clearly, change the position.

Shelf supports come in several sizes. Buy some of each to aid in stacking the kiln. When stacking, measure the supports with the pieces and stack to save space. Shelf supports should be used in threes and should be placed on each shelf at the same place.

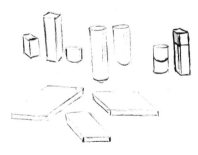

❦ The first firing, called a bisque fire, is done at low temperatures. If the clay does not need to be glazed, the ware needs only one firing; if the pieces are to be glazed, the bisque firing is important. Do not try to glaze ware when it is bone dry; not only is it difficult to do but the results are unpredictable in the fire. If the clay and glaze are to be fired to c/04, as an example, in the final firing first bisque to c/08, then glaze the pieces and refire to c/04.

❦ For bisque firing the ware can be stacked in the kiln close together. Pieces may touch or be placed inside each other to conserve space. In a glaze fire the pieces must not touch; if they do, they will be joined together when cooled. There is no exact measurement for this spacing; just be sure there is some distance, perhaps a quarter inch, between pieces.

❦ Stilts are not necessary if the feet of pottery or the bases of sculpture are first waxed. It is suggested that this method be used in schools; it will save a great deal of stacking time for the teacher.

❦ High school students can be taught to help with stacking the kiln as well as with the firing process. They should understand at this level that the kiln and firing are a part of the clay process and necessary for the completed form.

❧ Shelves and supports which will aid in stacking the kiln to its capacity can be bought in various sizes. Half shelves will help to take care of large pieces in combination with many more small pieces. Wasted space from poor stacking is money and time consuming, so stack carefully. A heavily stacked kiln may take more time to fire off, or finish, than a lightly stacked kiln, although there is no set time element. It is impossible to say, for example, that a c/04 kiln will take six hours to fire off. Time is dependent, in most cases, on the time it takes the kiln to reach certain temperatures.

❧ If the kiln is finished firing at 4 P.M., do not open it before the next morning, and then do so slowly. Open it about two inches and allow it to cool slowly, advancing the opening of the door as the kiln cools. Do not force cooling, because that is hard on the elements; sudden cold may snap hot electrical wires.

❧ Keep the kiln, as well as clay areas, clean. If glazes have dripped on kiln floors and shelves, clean them off after each firing; otherwise, they will melt in another fire and ruin other pieces. Kiln wash should be used at all times.

Classroom Organization

These are ideas which may help in the classroom organization; in turn, they will give both students and teacher more working time.

❧ Be sure desk tops are covered with newspapers or canvas. This will save

If a lot of ware is to be fired, place the ware to conserve space. Use the hand as a measuring device to find objects of the same height. In a bisque fire, pieces may be placed inside of each other and against each other. For a glaze fire the pieces may not touch.

Here is an example of stacking to conserve space.

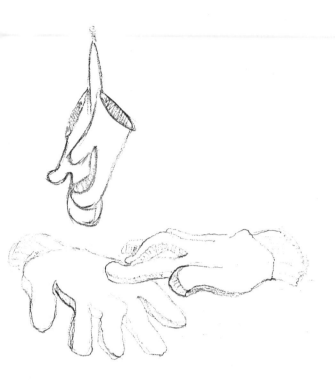

Use mittens or gloves to remove ware from a warm kiln. This prevents burned fingers, as well as the possibility of dropping a piece because it is too hot.

Cover desk tops with newspaper, plastic, or canvas. Have a plaster bat to work on or a heavy piece of cardboard if plaster is not available. However, cardboard does not work as well as plaster. A can for water or slip is necessary. Put extra clay in a plastic bag to keep it moist and workable.

cleaning time as well as preserve desk-top surfaces. Individual plaster bats make excellent working surfaces, and finished pieces need not be removed from them.

✤ If an explanation about some processes, etc. has to be given, be sure it is done before the clay itself is passed to the students, unless the students participate or work along with the teacher.

✤ Be sure clay is of working consistency. If time permits, prepare hand-size balls of clay, which can be passed out quickly. If no time is available for previous prepation, be sure each student receives a heaping handful to wedge his own ball. In either case, have sufficient clay left over in case some students need more clay to complete a piece. It is unwise to give students more clay than they may need; for it dries quickly, particularly if it has been worked in the hands a great deal. Small plastic bags or pieces of damp cloth will help the student keep his coils and excess clay in good condition at his desk.

✤ Be sure to have one area in the room which can be used for drying pieces. This does not necessarily mean out of the students' reach, but it should be an area that will not have to be used for several days, so that the pieces will not have to be moved.

❖ It is desirable for the teacher not to touch the student's piece or to have any other student handle it, especially in the wet stage. Therefore, it is best to allow each student to move his own piece to the area in the room reserved for drying. If the clay is picked up without a bat underneath it, there is always a chance of destroying the form by grasping it at the wrong place, dropping it, upsetting it, etc.

❖ Teachers often have a difficult time deciding which pieces should be fired. Explain carefully to students that each piece must be securely joined to withstand the fire. If the students understand this, then the teacher is free to select those pieces which he knows will survive. It is important that each child should have at least one piece successfully fired, even if he must try several times. If the kiln is small and it is difficult to find firing time, allow the student to have several clay experiences and then select one piece that he likes best to be fired.

❖ If running water and a sink are in the classroom, the cleaning-up job is not difficult. If there is no sink, several buckets of water with stacks of paper towels beside them in different sections of the room will help this job to be done quickly and easily. Desk tops can be sponged off. If the clay is of the proper consistency to work with, not sticky, that is, the job of cleaning is not as difficult as many people believe.

❖ If students make their own tools, the time for doing it will have to be deter-

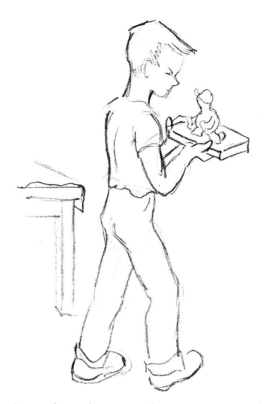

Let each student carry his own piece to the drying area.

If sinks are not available, a bucket of water, paper towels, and a wastepaper basket can be set in convenient areas throughout the room for easy cleanup.

mined by the teacher. Tools may be made after the student has had some experience with clay and knows what he would like to make, or they may be made while the student is working with clay and realizes his need. This will also depend on the student's age and level of ability. Fingers are, after all, the best tools.

❀ Be sure all tools and sponges are washed thoroughly after each use. Tools should be dried to prevent warping, molding, and rusting.

❀ Have each student sign his own piece after it is finished. If he has had little previous experience with clay, he will sometimes find it difficult to recognize his piece after the firing; for pieces shrink in size and change color. Signing the pieces is especially important with young children. The teacher also needs to study each piece with the individual student in mind.

❀ Dip feet or bases of pottery and sculpture into hot paraffin or paint with liquid wax. The pieces will not stick to the kiln floor, glaze will wipe off easily from the areas, and time will be saved in kiln stacking because stilts will be unnecessary. Actually, hot paraffin can be used on any area where glaze is not desirable.

❀ Keep all clay areas and working areas clean. Students should develop good work habits and understand that keeping these areas clean is as much a part of their art experience as creating.

Be sure each student signs his own work. First
initial and last name are the most helpful.

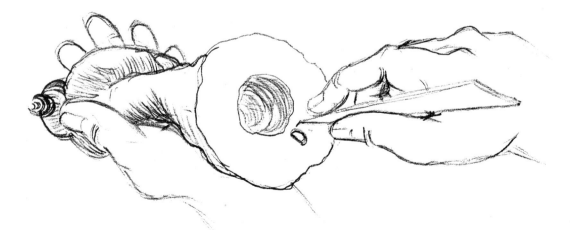

VIII IN CONCLUSION

The whole art of teaching is only the art of awakening the natural curiosity of young minds for the purpose of satisfying it afterwards.
ANATOLE FRANCE[1]

True value of this method of exploration, it seems to the author, lies in the fact that the student must take the first step, and this refers not only to the initial handling of the clay itself but to each succeeding move he makes toward his final solution. In other words, teaching starts with explaining and then helping the student to understand *what he is doing* rather than explaining and then telling him *what he should do*. By this method each student will be able to grow and develop at his own pace, which is based upon his ability and interest. Too many times the art experience is so dictated that the results achieved are not the students' own, but rather those that

[1] *The Daughter of Clémentine*, part II, chap. 4.

110

stem from what the teacher believes to be necessary.

For the teacher as well as the student the use of the hand-building method will be more than a way of working with clay. The object made will have an individuality and character determined by the maker. The amount of opportunity provided to explore and experience what clay will do can only enhance the experience to full satisfaction. It will always be revealing; for no one can touch clay and form with it without giving his mark of identity to the material and the piece he has formed, forever to be enjoyed and used. For others, these objects become a source of pleasure through "seeing" and "feeling," as well as through developing a perceptive understanding of the person who has made them. Indeed, all art is a matter of love. De Gourmont put it this way:[2] "Art is the accomplice of love. Take love away and there is no longer art."

It is hoped that teachers will lead their students through other experiences with other materials, such as wood and metal, which will supplement the sensory experiences they have had with clay. The approaches suggested here can be used, thereby continually developing the student's ability to understand himself and his way of working.

Wood carving experiences by students at Linden Hall Academy and Junior College.

[2] Remy De Gourmont, from "Decadence."

111

Bibliography

ARNHEIM, RUDOLF. *Art and Visual Perception*. Berkeley: University of California Press, 1954.

BENNETT, WENDELL C. *Ancient Arts of the Andes*. New York: Simon & Schuster, 1954.

Bible. Genesis, 2:7; Isaiah, 64:8; Jeremiah, 18:1–16; Job, 33:6; Psalms, 40:2; Romans, 9:21.

BINNS, CHARLES F. *The Potter's Craft*. 3d ed. Princeton, N. J.: D. Van Hostrand Co., 1955.

BLOSSFELT, KARL. *Art Forms in Nature*. Ser. 2. New York: E. Weyhe, 1932.

CANFIELD, RUTH. *The Pottery Shop*. New York: New York University, 1955.

COX, WARREN. *The Book of Pottery and Porcelain*. 2 vols. New York: Crown Publishers, Inc., 1944. 1 vol. ed., 1958.

DE FRANCESCO, ITALO L. *Art Education—Its Means and Ends*. New York: Harper & Bros., 1958.

DE SAGER, WALTER A. *Making Pottery*. London and New York: The Studio Publications, 1948.

DOUGLAS, FREDERIC H. & D'HARNONCOURT. *Indian Art of the United States*. New York: Simon & Schuster, 1941.

DUNCAN, JULIA HAMLIN, AND D'AMICO, VICTOR. *How to Make Pottery and Ceramic Sculpture*. New York: Simon & Schuster, 1947.

FEININGER, ANDREA. *The Anatomy of Nature*. New York: Crown Publishers, Inc., 1956.

GHISELIN, BREWSTER (ed.). *The Creative Process*. Berkeley: University of California Press, 1955.

HILDRETH, ELLEN STEPHENS. *Clay Modeling in the Classroom*. Springfield, Mass.: Milton Bradley Co., 1892.

HONEY, W. B. *The Art of the Potter*. New York: McGraw-Hill Book Co., Inc., 1946.

KENNY, JOHN B. *The Complete Book of Pottery Making*. New York: Greenberg: Publisher, Inc., 1949.

LEACH, BERNARD. *A Potter's Book*. London: Faker and Faker, 1946.

LOWENFELD, VIKTOR. *Creative and Mental Growth*. 3rd ed. New York: Macmillan Co., 1957.

MASON, J. ALDEN. *The Ancient Civilizations of Peru*. Baltimore, Md.: Penguin Books, Inc., 1957.

NORTON, F. H. *Ceramics for the Artist Potter*. Reading, Mass.: Addison-Wesley Publishing Co., Inc., 1956.

PEARL, RICHARD M. *How to Know the Minerals and Rocks*. New York: The New American Library (Signet Book) by arrangement with McGraw-Hill Book Co., Inc., 1957.

PRESCOTT, DANIEL ALFRED. *Emotion and the Educative Process*. Washington, D.C.: American Council on Education, 1938.

PUTNAM, BRENDA. *Animal X-rays*. New York: G. P. Putnam's Sons, 1947.

RANDALL, RUTH H. *Ceramic Sculpture*. New York: Watson-Guptill Publishers, Inc., 1948.

RHODES, DANIEL. *Clay and Glazes for the Potter*. New York: Greenberg: Publisher, Inc., 1957.

ROUSSEAU, JEAN JACQUES. *Emile*. Book 2. New York: E. P. Dutton & Co., 1911.

STITES, RAYMOND. *The Arts and Man*. New York: McGraw-Hill Book Co., Inc., 1940.

STRUPPECK, JULES. *The Creation of Sculpture*. New York: Henry Holt and Co., 1952.

TUROFF, MURIEL PARGH. *How to Make Pottery and Other Ceramic Ware*. New York: Crown Publishers, 1949.

TYLER, KEITH. *Pottery Without a Wheel*. Peoria, Ill.: Chas. A. Bennett Co., Inc., 1955.

VAILLANT, G. C. *The Aztecs of Mexico*. New York: Pelican Books, 1955.

VON HAGEN, VICTOR W. *Realm of the Incas*. New York: The New American Library (Mentor Book), 1957.

WICKISER, RALPH L. *An Introduction to Art Education*. Yonkers, N. Y.: World Book Co., 1957.

WREN, HENRY and DENISE. *Hand Craft Pottery*. London: Sir Isaac Pitman & Sons, 1933.

ZIM, HERBERT, and SHAFFER, PAUL R. *Rocks and Minerals*. New York: Simon & Schuster, 1957.

Film Libraries

The Pennsylvania State University
Audio-Visual Aids Library
University Park, Pennsylvania

Boston University Film Library
School of Education
332 Bay State Road
Boston 15, Massachusetts

Bailey Films
6509 De Longpre Avenue
Hollywood 28, California

Associated Films, Inc.
Broad at Elm
Ridgefield, New Jersey

United World Films, Inc.[1]
1445 Park Avenue
New York 29, New York

Modern Talking Picture Service, Inc.[1]
3 E. 54th Street
New York 20, New York

Indiana University[2]
Audio-Visual Center
Bloomington, Indiana

[1] Distributes an excellent film on the making of Lenox china.
[2] An excellent source of Adult Education material for working with clay.

Index